C O N T E N T S

Words that are explained in the glossary are printed in
SMALL CAPITALS the first time they are mentioned in the text.

◨ INTRODUCTION

Bangladesh was once part of the Indian state of Bengal. Hinduism flourished here for thousands of years before armies from Afghanistan brought Islam in the 1200s. In the 1500s, the Afghans were overthrown by another group of Moslem invaders, the Moguls, who had swept through northern India. In the 1700s, India was conquered by the British and became part of their world-wide empire. The British built roads and railways in Bengal, but few factories or schools.

In 1947, India became independent. A new country of Pakistan was created from the two parts of India where Moslems were in the majority. In this way, India became a homeland for Hindus and Pakistan a homeland for Moslems. The two parts of Pakistan were separated by nearly 3,000 kilometres of northern India. Bengal itself was split, with the western half remaining in India and the eastern half becoming East Pakistan. The British had built most of the

▼ *This government building is in the centre of Dhaka, the capital city. It was built by the British and combines British and Indian styles of architecture.*

COUNTRY FACT FILES

adesh

umming

YOUNG BOOKS

First published in 1999 by Macdonald Young Books
An imprint of Wayland Publishers Ltd
© Macdonald Young Books 1999

Macdonald Young Books
61 Western Road
Hove
East Sussex
BN3 1JD

Find Macdonald Young Books on the Internet at
http://www.myb.co.uk

Design and typesetting Roger Kohn Designs
Commissioning editor Rosie Nixon
Editor Merle Thompson
Picture research Gina Brown
Maps János Márffy

We are grateful to the following for permission
to reproduce photographs:
Front Cover: Axiom, above (Jim Holmes);
Panos, below (B Klass);
Axiom, pages 8/9 above (Jim Holmes), 14 (Jim Holmes),
24/25 above (Jim Holmes), 30 (Jim Holmes), 31 (Jim Holmes),
32 (Jim Holmes), 43 (Jim Holmes); Chapel Studios, pages 21
(Zul Mukhida), 29 (Zul Mukhida), 36 below (Zul Mukhida), 39
(Zul Mukhida), 40 (Zul Mukhida); David Cumming, pages 19,
33, 36 above; Ecoscene, page 18 below left; Eye Ubiquitous,
page 16 above left (David Cumming); Life File Ltd, page 20
below (Stuart Norgrove); Christine Osborne, page 38; Panos,
pages 8 below (Peter Barker), 11 (B Klass), 12 (Trygve
Bølstad), 13 centre left (Jim Holmes), 13 below left
(Z Nelson), 15 above left (Trygve Bølstad), 15 below left
(Jim Holmes), 16 below left (Mark McEvoy), 17 (Jim Holmes),
18 (Peter Backer), 20 above, 22 (Ron Giling), 23 (Ron Giling),
24 above (N Cooper & J Hammond), 26 above left (Peter
Barker), 26 (Zed Nelson) centre right, 27 (Ron Giling), 28
(Neil Cooper), 34 (B Klass), 35 (Trygve Bølstad), 37 (Peter
Barker), 42 (Jim Holmes); Science Photo Library, page 11
(CNES, 1990 Distribution Spot Image) above; Tony Stone,
pages 10 (Ann Jousfrie), 41 (Tim Davis).

The statistics given in this book are the most up to date
available at the time of going to press

Printed in Hong Kong by Wing King Tong

A CIP catalogue record for this book is available from
the British Library

ISBN: 0 7500 2618 9

▲ *Like all Bangladeshi children, these girls often have to walk several kilometres to school or to the shops, because there are few buses.*

BANGLADESH AT A GLANCE

● Area: 144,000 square kilometres
● Population (1996): 123 million
● Population density: 854 people per square kilometre
● Capital: Dhaka, population (1993) 6,105,500. It is estimated that, by 1995, it had risen to 7.8 million
● Other main cities (1993): Chittagong 2,000,000; Khulna 877,000; Rajshahi 517,000
● Highest point: Mowdok Mual, 1,003 metres
● Languages: Bangla (Bengali), English
● Major religions: Islam, Hinduism, Buddhism, Christianity
● Life expectancy at birth (1996): 56 years, compared with 76 years in the UK and USA
● Infant mortality (1996): 102 per 1,000 live births, compared with 6 per 1,000 in the UK and 8 in USA
● Literacy (1995): men 49%, women 26%
● Currency: Taka = 100 paise
● Economy: highly dependent on agriculture, with a low level of industrialization
● Major resources: good farming land, timber, fish
● Major products: clothes, prawns and frogs' legs, jute, tea, leather, rice, newsprint
● Environmental problems: sewage and industrial waste have damaged inland and coastal waters

factories in the western half, so East Pakistan was left with little industry.

Although united by religion, West and East Pakistan soon became bitter enemies. For the East, rule by West Pakistan seemed to have replaced rule by the British. The final blow came in 1970, when the East's Sheikh Mujibur Rahman was not allowed to be Prime Minister after winning the elections. Talks to settle the issue broke down and, on 26 March 1971, Sheikh Mujibur Rahman announced that the East would become an independent country. After a brief period of conflict, Bangladesh came into existence on 16 December 1971. It was now totally separate from West Pakistan, which was renamed Pakistan.

Bangladesh started out with many political and economic disadvantages. A succession of natural disasters and bad governments has made its struggle to overcome them more difficult. Undeterred, its tough people have been determined to win through. They have been rewarded by improvements that would have challenged much richer nations, let alone one of the poorest.

THE LANDSCAPE

◀ *Water is an important part of the landscape of Bangladesh. This photograph shows people washing in one of the many rivers that criss-cross the country. The main rivers are marked on the map below. The Ganges and Brahmaputra are the biggest by far.*

Bangladesh occupies part of the north-eastern corner of the Indian SUBCONTINENT. It is surrounded by India, apart from a short border with Myanmar (Burma) and its 580-kilometre coastline. Most of the coastline is not continuous, but broken up by the channels of a delta. The rivers Ganges, Brahmaputra and Meghna flow through the delta and empty into the Bay of Bengal in the Indian Ocean. The Ganges and the Brahmaputra start in the Himalaya Mountains; the Ganges in India and the Brahmaputra in Tibet, China. In Bangladesh, the Ganges is renamed the Padma and the Brahmaputra becomes the Jamuna. Together they drain 2,500,000 square kilometres of land. Only the River Amazon and its tributaries carry more water to the sea. But no other RIVER SYSTEM transports so much silt. The waters of the Ganges and Brahmaputra contain over two billion tonnes. Although the River Meghna contributes its share of silt to the total load, it is insignificant compared to that of the

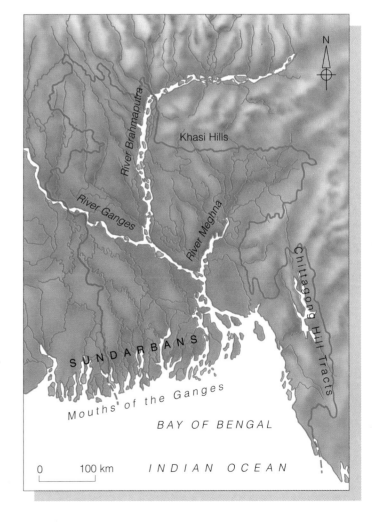

River Brahmaputra

Khasi Hills

River Ganges

River Meghna

Chittagong Hill Tracts

SUNDARBANS

Mouths of the Ganges

BAY OF BENGAL

0   100 km   INDIAN OCEAN

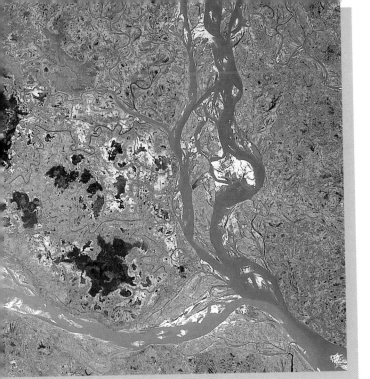

◀ *The Ganges (left) and Brahmaputra rivers viewed from space.*

the hills in the north-east and south-east.

Bangladesh is very open, with clumps of trees dotting the landscape and lining the river banks. Only about 15 per cent of the land is covered with forests. These are on the Chittagong Hill Tracts in the south-east and in the Sundarbans in the south-west. Covering about 6,000 square kilometres, the Sundarbans stretches 80 kilometres inland and over the border into India. Much of the Sundarbans is marshy land which is covered by water at high tide.

other two rivers.

All this silt is dropped as the rivers enter the Bay of Bengal. Over the centuries, this has built up to form the land on which the people of Bangladesh live. The land is very flat and low because of the way in which it has been created. The highest points are

▲ *The Sundarbans, the world's largest river-mouth forest.*

KEY FACTS

● Bangladesh means 'land of the Bangla-speaking people', from Bangla, the local language, and desh, land.
● More than 75% of Bangladesh is less than 10 metres above sea level.
● Bangladesh is the same size as England and Northern Ireland, or the American state of Illinois.
● Bangladesh is the largest delta in the world.
● The channel of the combined Rivers Padma, Jamuna and Meghna is 25-kilometres wide at one point near the main mouth.
● Rain water from an area of land nearly the size of India drains into these three rivers.

11

◀ Heavy flooding turns Bangladesh into an inland sea and life comes to a standstill. The devastation can be enormous. People, animals, homes and roads are washed away.

Bangladesh lies across the Tropic of Cancer, so it has a tropical climate. The year is divided up into four seasons: autumn (October–November), winter (December–February), summer (March–May) and rainy (June–September). It is humid and hot all the year round. During the winter, temperatures drop to a pleasant 20°C, while in the summer they can reach an uncomfortable 35°C.

It is driest between October and May, and wettest between June and September. Three times as much rain falls then as in all the other eight months combined. This rain is brought by winds, called the monsoon, which blow in from the Indian Ocean.

The monsoon usually starts in the middle of June. It is an unpredictable wind. Sometimes it comes early, sometimes late; some years it brings too much rain and other years too little. When there is a lot of rain, Bangladesh's rivers do not have the capacity to drain it all away and they burst their banks to flood the adjoining land. These floods do little damage because

they are shallow and do not extend far. More serious flooding occurs when the monsoon's rain starts two or three weeks early. Then, its arrival coincides with the water from the snow and ice melting in the Himalayas. The volume of water in the rivers is so great that the resulting floods are catastrophic.

The rainy season also brings fierce tropical storms, called cyclones, which form out in the Bay of Bengal. With winds of up to 200 kilometres per hour, cyclones cause havoc on the coast, flattening everything in their way.

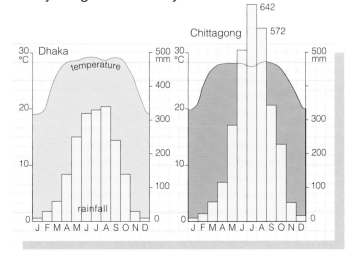

KEY FACTS

● The monsoon brings 80% of Bangladesh's annual rainfall.

● About 60% of Bangladesh's rice is grown during the monsoon season.

● On 30 April 1991, a severe cyclone killed between 140,000 and 200,000 people, when very strong winds and a 7-metre-high tidal wave hit the coast.

As the winds push the sea into the shallows near the shore, towering tidal waves can rear up and crash down on the land, adding to the damage.

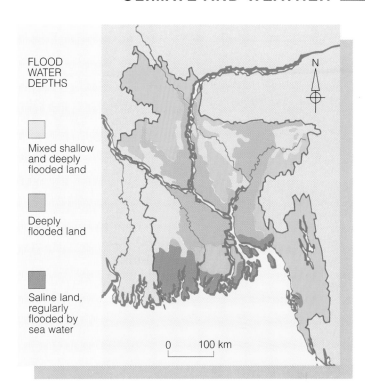

FLOOD WATER DEPTHS

Mixed shallow and deeply flooded land

Deeply flooded land

Saline land, regularly flooded by sea water

0   100 km

◀ *Strong shelters have been built on high ground. Whole villages can use them to escape floods and high winds.*

▶ *These workmen are strengthening a river embankment before the arrival of the monsoon rains.*

NATURAL RESOURCES

Bangladesh has few natural resources. In the north-west, near Rangpur, there are large deposits of limestone that are used to make cement, FERTILIZERS and chemicals.

There are several small natural gas fields, the most recent of which were opened in 1994. Gas is piped from Sylhet to a nearby fertilizer factory, as well as to Dhaka and Chittagong. Small amounts of oil are also extracted near Sylhet. At Jamalgang, in the north-west, coal is mined, but not in large quantities.

In common with most developing countries, Bangladesh is short of electricity. The south-east is powered by hydro-electricity from a dam across the River Karnaphuli. It provides about 10 per cent of Bangladesh's total electricity. The rest is generated by power stations burning either oil or gas. Since Bangladesh's own supplies are insufficient for this, they have to be topped up with foreign oil. Importing it is expensive, and as a result there is little money to build more power stations.

Bangladesh's forests have always been an important natural resource because they have provided wood for building homes and for cooking. Their timber is also used for making paper. In 1995, Bangladesh produced 83,000 tonnes of paper. This was enough for its own needs and for selling abroad. Much of it came from a large mill in Khulna, which is supplied by the forests of the Sundarbans. High-quality teak grows on the Chittagong Hill Tracts. It is made into furniture in local

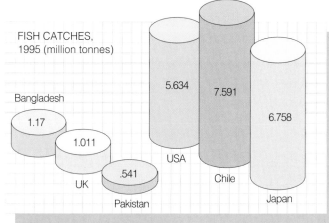

FISH CATCHES, 1995 (million tonnes)

Bangladesh 1.17
UK 1.011
Pakistan .541
USA 5.634
Chile 7.591
Japan 6.758

◀ *Bangladesh's many rivers provide its villagers with a plentiful supply of fish.*

▶ *Bamboo being floated down the River Karnaphuli to Chittagong, where it is made into furniture.*

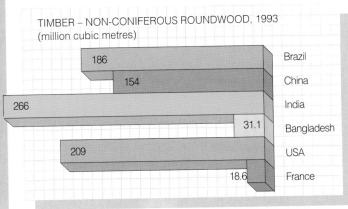

▲ *The soil around Dhaka is good for making bricks. The sun is hot enough to dry them out, ready for use.*

KEY FACTS

● Building a dam across the River Karnaphuli created a 689-square kilometre lake.

● In 1993–94 prawns and frogs' legs, together, earned Bangladesh US$ 198m. After jute and clothes, they were the third best exports.

● In 1994, each person in Bangladesh used the energy equivalent to 65 kilograms of oil a year, compared with 3,754 kilograms in the UK and 7,905 kilograms in the USA.

factories, as well as being exported.

Recently, the sea has helped to create a thriving export industry – prawn farming. Prawns are bred in lagoons along the coast and in flooded fields by the side of the tidal parts of the rivers. Farmers earn more from prawns than rice, so they turn their fields into seawater ponds. Now frogs are also being farmed in ponds because their legs are in demand as a luxury food abroad.

TIMBER – NON-CONIFEROUS ROUNDWOOD, 1993
(million cubic metres)

Brazil	186
China	154
India	266
Bangladesh	31.1
USA	209
France	18.6

Bangladesh is a very crowded place. The population has trebled in the last fifty years. In the late 1940s, there were 290 people per square kilometre, now there are over 850. There are several reasons for this alarming increase.

Bangladesh has a limited welfare system, so parents have needed children to look after them in old age. However, poor healthcare and a bad diet mean that many children die young. Parents in rural areas have a lot of children to ensure that some of them will reach adulthood. In a poor country like Bangladesh, parents also consider children to be valuable assets. Children can earn money and, the more

◀ *Today, parents in the cities generally have only one or two children.*

▶ *These hill tribe people live deep in the forests, away from everyone else. Their survival is being threatened by logging companies, who want to cut down the trees for timber.*

there are, the better-off a family will be. This has meant that there has been a high birth-rate and families have been large.

Since Bangladesh has few industries, the majority of people have to work on the land. The amount of land is fixed but the number of Bangladeshis who want to use it has increased enormously. The problem is made worse by the laws of inheritance and an unfair distribution of land.

LAND SHORTAGES

When a farmer dies, his land has to be divided up between his children (with sons, according to custom, receiving a larger

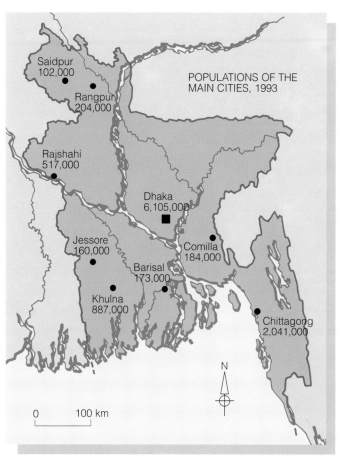

POPULATIONS OF THE MAIN CITIES, 1993

Saidpur 102,000

Rangpur 204,000

Rajshahi 517,000

Dhaka 6,105,000

Jessore 160,000

Comilla 184,000

Barisal 173,000

Khulna 887,000

Chittagong 2,041,000

N

0   100 km

share than daughters). Consequently, as farmland is passed down through the generations, it is divided up into smaller and smaller plots. Having a large number of children results in even smaller farms. Today, 50 per cent of farmers possess less than 0.2 hectares of land (roughly the size of a tennis court). They can grow enough food to feed their families, but there is nothing left over to sell to provide an income. Their only option is to work for a large landowner. These are few in number, but they own a lot of land. Currently, 5 per cent of the population owns 25 per cent of the land.

◄ *The cities' slums are bursting with people, which means that families live in very crowded conditions.*

Many of these landowners have thousands of hectares of land, which makes them rich and powerful. Most of them abuse their power, paying their workers little and hiring and firing them at will. As they only need workers for a few months of the year, to help with the planting and harvesting of crops, a small farmer cannot rely on them for a regular income, however little.

Even if a small farmer can obtain some extra land for growing crops to sell, the monsoon or a cyclone can destroy his harvest within minutes. He is then forced to borrow from a moneylender at a very high rate of INTEREST. It is easy to run up a debt which will take years to repay. Many small farmers find it impossible to survive in the countryside.

OVERCROWDED CITIES

Every year, 5 per cent of the rural population leaves the countryside. This means that nearly 5 million villagers arrive annually in Bangladesh's cities. These new arrivals want homes and jobs, both of which are already in short supply. Most end up working part-time, doing badly paid odd-jobs for a few days a month. Home for them is a leaky shack in one of the shanty towns on the edge of a city. Here, conditions are cramped and dirty, and disease is common.

Bangladesh's cities, especially Dhaka, have been changing as fast as they have been growing. Most of these developments,

▲ *The richest people live in Dhaka. Their houses are hidden behind walls and protected by strong gates.*

◄ *Dhaka is a city of great contrasts. This luxury hotel overlooks the shabby homes of some of the poorest inhabitants.*

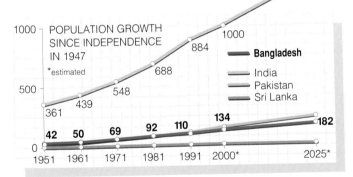

A busy street market in the heart of Dhaka. Men usually go to the market to shop as women are expected to stay in the home.

POPULATION GROWTH SINCE INDEPENDENCE IN 1947

*estimated

Bangladesh
India
Pakistan
Sri Lanka

1951	1961	1971	1981	1991	2000*	2025*
361	439	548	688	884	1000	1400
42	50	69	92	110	134	182

KEY FACTS

● In 1993, there was 1 doctor for every 12,884 people in Bangladesh. In the UK, there was 1 doctor for every 300 people, while in the USA there was 1 doctor for every 421 people.

● More than 13 million people live in shanty towns around the main cities.

● In Bangladesh, each woman has an average of 4 children. In the UK, each woman has an average of 1.8 children, while in the USA the average is 2.1 children.

● The population of Bangladesh is increasing by 1.8% a year, compared with 0.3% in the UK and 0.9% in the USA.

● There are 94 women for every 100 men in Bangladesh. In the UK and the USA, there are 105 women for every 100 men.

● There are 10 million farms in Bangladesh, which have been split up into 59,850,000 plots of land.

however, have benefited the rich rather than the poor, who cannot afford satellite television or luxury hotels.

A NATION OF VILLAGES

Although millions have moved to the cities, Bangladesh remains a rural nation. It has 70,000 villages, where nearly 85 per cent of the population live.

Village life has changed little over the years. It revolves around the farming calendar. Men work in the fields looking after their crops and animals, while women stay at home, preparing meals and taking

care of the children and other household matters. Few homes have running water and electricity.

TRIBAL GROUPS

Bangladesh has twenty tribal groups, including the Chakma, Khasi and Manipuri peoples. They make up less than 1 per cent of the total population and they farm on the hills of the north-east and south-east. They keep themselves separate so that they can preserve their centuries-old cultures and customs.

DAILY LIFE

RELIGION

Most Bangladeshis are Moslems and Islam plays a prominent part in their daily lives. This is most obvious in the treatment of women. In Islam, males are given the dominant role in society. Husbands are expected to work to support their families. Wives are expected to stay at home; even going out alone is discouraged. This division of responsibilities results in women being dependent on men, both financially and socially.

EDUCATION

The different treatment of men and women in Bangladesh begins when children are very young. Since girls are not meant to work, parents consider educating them properly a waste of time. Few girls are sent to secondary school, even though the government pays for most of the cost. As a result, 74 per cent of adult women can neither read nor write. This places them at

▲ **Strolling on the beach. This middle-class city family can afford a seaside holiday at the popular resort of Cox's Bazaar, south of Chittagong.**

▼ **These city children are fortunate to have some waste land near their homes to use for sports.**

PERCENTAGE OF PUPILS ATTENDING PRIMARY SCHOOLS, 1990 (ages 6-11)

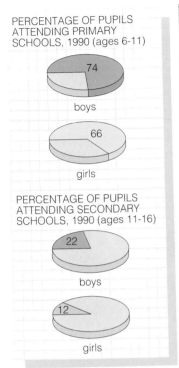

74 boys

66 girls

PERCENTAGE OF PUPILS ATTENDING SECONDARY SCHOOLS, 1990 (ages 11-16)

22 boys

12 girls

a great disadvantage — as well as giving men more power over them.

In Bangladesh as a whole, 62 per cent of adults are illiterate. This is a reflection of the poverty there. Poor families cannot afford to let their children go to school instead of working. Although primary schools are free, only 70 per cent of eligible pupils attend them. Of these children, only 25 per cent will complete five years of basic education.

Overall, the best educated people in Bangladesh are generally men from rich families. Not only do these families appreciate the importance of a good education, they can afford to send their children to school.

EMPOWERING WOMEN

In Bangladesh, raising the status of women is being taken very seriously. It has been recognized that their social inferiority has been one of the stumbling blocks to

▲ *There are not enough schools, so classrooms are usually crammed with pupils.*

progress. 'Empowering women' means giving them the means to influence and make decisions. In Bangladesh, this has involved women being taught how to read and write, being given information on contraception, and being encouraged to form WORKERS' CO-OPERATIVES. Female empowerment has been effective. For example, as more parents are using contraceptives, and the size of families has

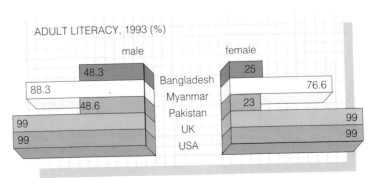

ADULT LITERACY, 1993 (%)

	male	female
Bangladesh	48.3	25
Myanmar	88.3	76.6
Pakistan	48.6	23
UK	99	99
USA	99	99

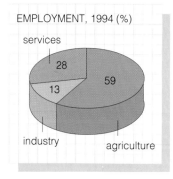

▲ *This young boy is helping his family by working. He is breaking stones for a new road.*

EMPLOYMENT, 1994 (%)

services 28

13

59

industry

agriculture

dropped, the population has been growing at a slower rate. With less mouths to feed, Bangladesh has more money available to modernize. Girls, too, are being given a better education.

Inevitably, the empowerment of women has its critics. Most of these are men who think that it is damaging Islam. In 1993, Taslima Nasreen caused an uproar when she wrote about the oppression of women in her book Lajja (Shame). She had to flee Bangladesh, but she has since returned home to continue the fight for equal rights for women.

HEALTH PROBLEMS

Classes in health and hygiene are also playing a part in the empowerment of women. Since the majority of women have received little education, they are unaware of even the simplest matters connected with taking care of their own and their children's health. Water can easily spread disease, so in a country where there are a lot of rivers, illnesses spread quickly. Sanitation is poor. There is a lack of sewage and water-treatment plants, toilets

KEY FACTS

● In 1995, there were 84 newspapers in Bangladesh for every 1,000 homes. In the UK, there were 108 newspapers for every 1,000 homes, and in the USA, 104.

● In the same year, there were 83 televisions and 80 radios for every 1,000 homes in Bangladesh. In the UK, there were 105 televisions and 110 radios for every 1,000 homes, while in the USA there were 111 televisions and 123 radios.

● In 1993, there were 2 telephones for every 1,000 people in Bangladesh. In the UK, there were 494 telephones for every 1,000 people, and in the USA, 574.

● 50% of houses are made of mud bricks and are without plumbing: one toilet may be shared by as many as 50 families.

● In 1994, 40% of married couples used contraception, compared with 19% in 1983.

● In Bangladesh, 5% of managers are women while, in the UK, 33% are managers, and in the USA, 42%.

● Education is free at government schools for all 6 to 14 year olds.

and running water in homes. This means that the rivers are full of germs. Yet this is the water people have to use for washing. Telling women about the dirty water, together with giving them advice on how to keep food clean and to improve their diet, is helping to prevent illnesses. In the end, this will give people better and longer lives. Even so, Bangladesh is still short of the doctors and hospitals it needs to improve things further.

LEISURE

The arrival of satellite television is helping to undermine many long-held family values. Bangladeshi teenagers can now see how their contemporaries behave in other countries. This is making them question their own way of life. However, this is confined to the cities. In the countryside, few people can afford televisions. Their favourite pastime is

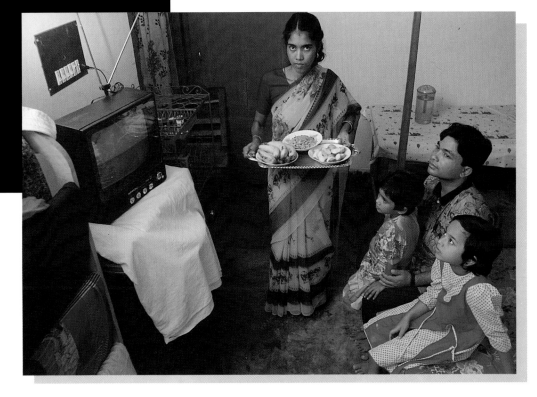

▶ *In the cities, satellite television is giving people new ideas that are worrying the older generation.*

▲ *The Hindu festival of Bera is celebrated with boat races between local villages.*

watching a much bigger screen – in cinemas. The most common films are action-packed musicals whose catchy songs can be heard blaring out of radios everywhere. Football is the most popular sport, followed by volleyball and kabadi (a team game like tag). Children possess few things to play with, apart from kites and toys made from bits and pieces they have found.

THE EXTENDED FAMILY

Considering all the obstacles to survival in Bangladesh, it is not surprising that the family as a group is important. By sticking together, it can survive tragedies which would defeat people on their own. In Bangladesh the family always comes before the individual, and many customs and practices ensure that this continues. For example, it is normal for several

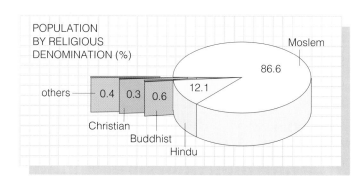

POPULATION BY RELIGIOUS DENOMINATION (%)

Moslem 86.6

others 0.4

0.3

0.6

12.1

Christian

Buddhist

Hindu

FESTIVALS AND HOLIDAYS

1 January	NEW YEAR'S DAY		1 May	MAY DAY
(The date changes each year)	RAMADAN (A period of fasting) Moslems mark the occasion when the Koran was revealed to the Prophet Muhammad. The date of Ramadan varies each year as it is based on the Moslem lunar calendar. Ramadan begins with the festival of JAMAT-UL-WIDA and ends with the ID-UL-FITR holiday		May/June	BUDDHA PURINIMA A Buddhist festival when the Buddha's birthday and his enlightenment are celebrated
			9 May	MUHARRAM (The Moslem New Year)
			18 July	ID-E-MILAD-UN-NABI A Moslem festival celebrating the birthday of the Prophet Muhammad
February	SARASWATI PUJA A Hindu festival in honour of Saraswati, goddess of knowledge		August/ September	HINDU BERA A Hindu festival when models of the bera (a bird which is half falcon, half peacock) are put on small rafts, set on fire and floated down rivers in honour of the god
21 February	NATIONAL MOURNING DAY A holiday in memory of those who died fighting West Pakistan in the early 1970s			
March	HOLI (The Festival of Colours) A Hindu festival celebrating the end of winter		September/ October	DUSSEHRA A Hindu festival celebrating Lord Rama's defeat of the demon-king, Ravanna DURGA PUJA A Hindu festival when images of the goddess Durga are put into rivers
March/April	GOOD FRIDAY AND EASTER MONDAY A Christian festival marking the death and resurrection of Jesus Christ		October/ November	DIWALI The Festival of Lights, when Hindus mark Lord Rama's return from exile
26 March	INDEPENDENCE DAY A holiday in memory of the day on which Bangladesh declared itself separate from West Pakistan		7 November	NATIONAL REVOLUTION DAY A holiday celebrating the beginning of Bangladesh's separation from former West Pakistan
14 April	PAHELA BAISAKH A Hindu festival celebrating the Bengali New Year		16 December	BIGANJ DIBASH (Victory Day) A holiday marking the end of the independence war with West Pakistan
18 April	ID-UL-ADHA (The Feast of the Sacrifice) A Moslem festival when sheep and goats are slaughtered and given to the poor and when the traditional pilgrimage to Mekka (the Haj) begins		25 December	CHRISTMAS DAY
			26 December	BOXING DAY holiday

◄ The cool marble floor of this mosque makes it a pleasant place for a chat after worship.

generations to live together under one roof as an 'extended' family. Children are brought up to respect their elders, and to consult their parents and the head of the family before making any important decisions, including who they will marry. After his wedding, a son does not leave home. Instead he brings his bride back to join his family. A young married couple, or indeed a single person, living on their own is very rare.

FESTIVALS AND HOLIDAYS

The two most important religious occasions are the Id-ul-Fitr and Id-ul-Adha festivals of Islam. The former marks the end of Ramadan (the month when Moslems fast). People dress in their best clothes to visit friends and family and give presents to children. Id-ul-Adha is the time when the annual pilgrimage to the holy city of Mekka, in Saudi Arabia, begins. Sheep and goats are killed and the meat given to the poor. The major festivals of the other religions are also celebrated by many people.

The main non-religious holidays are Independence Day and Victory Day. Both are connected with Bangladesh's fight to separate from West Pakistan.

RULE AND LAW

◄ **The modern Parliament in Dhaka.**

▼ **Sheikh Hasina Wajed, the Prime Minister of Bangladesh and leader of the Awami League.**

Bangladesh is a parliamentary democracy, with a written constitution. Its single-chamber Parliament, the Jatiya Sangsad in Dhaka, has 330 members, 300 of whom are elected. The other 30 seats are reserved for women, who are appointed by the 300 elected members. The elections for Parliament are held every five years, and people have to be aged over 18 to vote.

The Members of Parliament elect the President, who is the head of state. The President, too, is elected for a five-year term of office. He is responsible for appointing the chief justice and judges, including those who sit in the Supreme Court. He is also in charge of the armed forces.

The President appoints the Prime Minister, the head of the government. He or she is usually the leader of the political party with the largest number of seats in the Parliament. The Prime Minister governs Bangladesh with the help of a cabinet of ministers.

Bangladesh is divided up into four divisions for local government purposes: Chittagong, Dhaka, Khulna and Rajshahi. They are subdivided into zillas (districts),

PARLIAMENT (Jatiya Sangsad)
elected for a 5-year term
300 seats

Members of Parliament select 30 women for reserved seats

THE GOVERNMENT
Prime Minister
The Council of Ministers

THE PRESIDENT (elected for a 5-year term)

appoints Judges

appoints

controls The Armed Forces

THE ELECTORATE VOTES EVERY 5 YEARS

thanas (groups of unions) and unions (groups of villages), with elected councils at each level.

During its short life, Bangladesh has rarely functioned as a democracy and has

26

KEY FACTS

- In the national flag, the green background represents the greenery, vitality and youthfulness of Bangladesh. The red circle symbolizes the rising sun of independence after the dark night of a bloody struggle.
- Bangladesh is a member of the United Nations, the Non-Aligned Movement and the Organization of the Islamic Conference.
- The main political parties are the Awami League (socialist), the Bangladesh Nationalist Party (right of centre) and the National Party (a coalition of five parties keen on Islam playing a more important part in Bangladesh).
- At least 60% of Bangladeshis do not own any land. Governments have promised to break up large farms and redistribute their land, but rich landowners have always been able to stop them.
- It was only in 1996 that women were given the right to vote in elections.

FOOD AND FARMING

FLOODS AND THE SOIL

Bangladesh has in its favour a landscape with fertile soil suitable for farming. The silt deposited by rivers is rich in the nutrients that crops need in order to grow. Furthermore, the nutrients are topped up every year when the rivers flood and leave behind a new layer of silt in the fields. Thus the flooding, which can cause so much damage, also does good, provided it is not too deep to wash away all the silt. Consequently, Bangladesh has some of the world's best farming land.

THE IMPORTANCE OF FARMING

Farming remains the most important activity in Bangladesh. It is responsible for 25 per cent of all the wealth created there every year. About 65 per cent of the total labour force works in farming, or in jobs closely connected with it. Nearly 25 per cent of Bangladesh's EXPORT EARNINGS come from farming.

FOOD AND CASH CROPS

The two main crops, rice and jute, thrive in Bangladesh's hot, wet climate.

Rice is the main food crop. In fact, Bangladesh is one of the world's largest producers of rice. About 80 per cent of all farmland is used for growing it, and this land provides enough rice to feed the people. Wheat, potatoes, PULSES and a wide selection of fruit and vegetables are also cultivated to eat.

Most of the rice is planted in June and July and harvested after the monsoon, in December and January. Farmers who are able to irrigate their fields, by pumping water out of rivers or tube wells, can cultivate a second crop during the dry

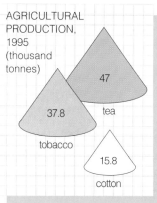

Young boys are catching fish that have been driven up to this wooden fence across a small river.

AGRICULTURAL PRODUCTION, 1995 (thousand tonnes)

- 47 tea
- 37.8 tobacco
- 15.8 cotton

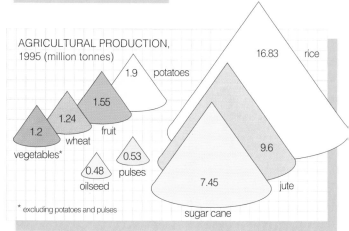

AGRICULTURAL PRODUCTION, 1995 (million tonnes)

- 16.83 rice
- 1.9 potatoes
- 1.55 fruit
- 1.24 wheat
- 1.2 vegetables*
- 0.48 oilseed
- 0.53 pulses
- 9.6 jute
- 7.45 sugar cane

* excluding potatoes and pulses

season. They plant the rice in December and January and harvest it in May and June. The dry season is also the time when farmers grow other food crops, like wheat and pulses, which do not like wet conditions. These are planted in November and December and harvested in March.

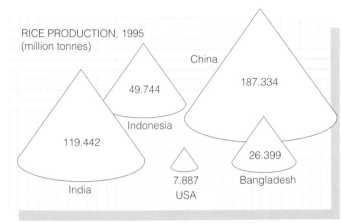

RICE PRODUCTION, 1995
(million tonnes)

China
187.334

Indonesia
49.744

India
119.442

USA
7.887

Bangladesh
26.399

Jute is the biggest cash crop. Its cultivation was expanded during British rule because it was wanted for making sacks, ropes and the backing material for carpets. Today, 25 million people are involved in growing, processing and selling jute. It is a major export-earner, second only to clothes. In recent years, however, it is becoming less important. Competition from man-made fibres is reducing the demand for jute world-wide. Since 1991, 22,000 jobs have been lost as a result of the government closing jute mills.

▼ *Young rice plants are being planted in 'nurseries'. They will be transferred to paddy-fields when they are bigger. Notice the wet conditions.*

The World Bank is giving the industry US$ 250 million to modernize. This money is being used to buy machinery for making high-quality jute yarn, which is wanted by carpet makers in Turkey and Iran. Hopefully, this will prevent further mill closures.

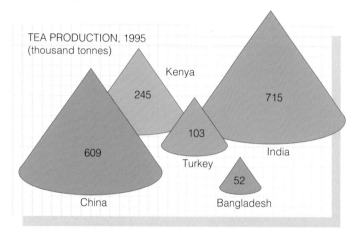

TEA PRODUCTION, 1995
(thousand tonnes)

Kenya
245

Turkey
103

India
715

China
609

Bangladesh
52

Tea is the second most valuable cash crop. It is grown on hillside plantations around the northern town of Sylhet. Cotton, sugar-cane and tobacco are the other cash crops.

THE GREEN REVOLUTION

During the 1970s and 1980s, new high-yielding varieties of rice were introduced. The size of harvests was significantly increased. This was called the Green Revolution. It allowed farmers to increase rice production so that there was plenty to

▼ *Tea pickers on a hillside plantation near Sylhet. Most of the crop will be exported.*

◀ *Bangladesh's climate and soil are good for growing a wide selection of vegetables, shown here in a local market.*

eat. Unfortunately, these varieties needed large amounts of expensive chemical fertilizers and PESTICIDES to be successful. Many poor rice farmers ended up in debt and had to sell their land.

FOOD AND DRINK

Since rice is plentiful, it is eaten every day. The most popular dishes are pulao and biryani. Pulao is boiled rice mixed up with spiced vegetables like onions, peas and carrots. Biryani is rice containing meat or chicken. As meat is expensive, only wealthy families have it regularly. Fish, on the other hand, is common because people can catch it for free. Even if they have to

buy fish, there are so many in the rivers that it is cheap. Moslems are forbidden to eat pork and pork products, and to drink alcohol, so these are not available in Bangladesh. People have tea and soft drinks when they are thirsty.

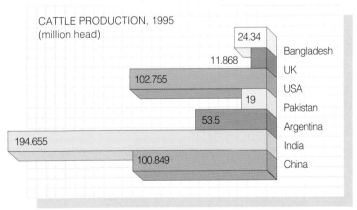

CATTLE PRODUCTION, 1995 (million head)

Country	Million head
Bangladesh	24.34
UK	11.868
USA	102.755
Pakistan	19
Argentina	53.5
India	194.655
China	100.849

■ TRADE AND INDUSTRY

Industry provides only 10 per cent of the wealth created every year in Bangladesh. It employs only 14 per cent of all workers.

PAST AND PRESENT PROBLEMS

A combination of factors has held back the development of Bangladesh's industries.

To start with, there are physical hindrances. Bangladesh lacks the natural resources and energy that industries need. The climate and the landscape make communications difficult. The delta is criss-crossed by rivers that require expensive bridges if journeys are to be made shorter. Floods frequently make travel impossible.

History, both past and present, must also share some of the blame. The British did not want Bangladesh to industrialize and compete with British factories back home.

▲ *Jute has to be soaked in water before the fibres can be extracted.*

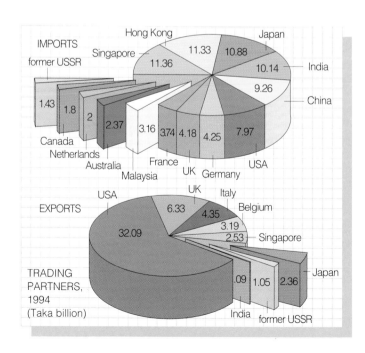

IMPORTS

Hong Kong 11.33
Japan 10.88
Singapore 11.36
former USSR 1.43
Canada 1.8
Netherlands 2
Australia 2.37
Malaysia 3.16
France 3.74
UK 4.18
Germany 4.25
USA 7.97
India 10.14
China 9.26

EXPORTS

USA 32.09
UK 6.33
Italy 4.35
Belgium 3.19
Singapore 2.53
Japan 2.36
former USSR 1.05
India .09

TRADING PARTNERS, 1994 (Taka billion)

They built mills to process jute, only because this made it easier to transport. West Pakistan behaved in a similar way after 1947, and blocked all its fellow countrymen's efforts at modernization. Since its own independence, Bangladesh has been badly governed. As a result, the jute industry established by the British, dominated the economy until recently. This was true both in terms of people employed and the amount earned from exports.

THE CLOTHING INDUSTRY

In the late 1970s, the government encouraged the textile industry to expand. By 1983, there were 47 factories, and by 1995 there were 2,100. Bangladesh had become the seventh largest clothes supplier to the USA and the main manufacturer of T-shirts and shirts for the European Union's member-countries. Although it does not employ as many people as the jute industry, the clothing industry now earns about four times as much money from exports as jute. The only problem is that Bangladesh has to import much of what it needs to make clothes, from cotton to buttons and zips, as well as the machinery. This added expense is cancelled out by the savings made from low wages.

CHEAP LABOUR

Its large population inevitably means that Bangladesh has a huge labour force. So great is the supply of workers, that factory owners can get away with paying them very low wages. There is, however, always someone willing to accept the wages the employers are offering. Many of these workers are children from poor families, desperately in need of money. Children are employed because they are cheaper than adults and complain less, and put up with working long hours in bad conditions. Working conditions are, however, improving, thanks to pressure from abroad. The government has recently introduced laws to ensure that working children are better treated.

◄ *This small shipbuilding yard near Dhaka builds passenger river boats.*

▶ *This is one of the many factories in Dhaka where clothes are made for export.*

INDUSTRIAL CENTRES

Most industries are located in Chittagong, which has the only oil refinery and steel mill in Bangladesh. It also has factories for freezing and tinning food, tanning leather and turning it into goods like handbags and wallets, for refining sugar, and making cement, machine tools and cigarettes.

Dhaka is the most important industrial city after Chittagong. It is the centre of the jute and clothing industries. Khulna, the third largest industrial city, has jute and paper mills, as well as cold storage and fish-freezing factories. Sylhet also produces paper, as well as processing tea and limestone, which is needed for making cement.

TRADE AND AID

Most of Bangladesh's imports come in through Chittagong, while the majority of exports leave via the port of Mongla.

The main exports are: clothes; jute and jute products; frozen prawns and frogs' legs; leather and leather goods. The USA, Western Europe, Singapore and Japan buy the bulk of them.

The main imports are: factory machinery; textiles; yarn to make clothing; petrol and oil. Most of them come from Singapore, Hong Kong, Japan, India and China.

Since Bangladesh has few industries, it is difficult for it to earn enough money from trade to survive without outside help. Between 1971 and 1995, US$ 26 billion has been pumped into Bangladesh to aid its economy. Most of this money has been loaned on the understanding that it will be repaid with interest. This is usually

KEY FACTS

● The textile factories make 90 different types of clothes.
● Skilled textile workers currently earn £30–60 (US$ 50–100) per month.
● In 1995, Bangladesh owed US$ 15.7 billion. In the same year it earned US$ 2.7 billion from exports. But it had to spend US$ 4.7 billion on imports, like machinery, to help make the things to export.
● In 1994–95, US$ 1.2 billion was sent back by Bangladeshis working abroad.

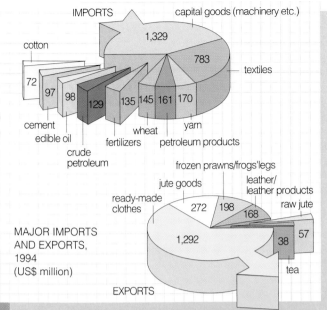

IMPORTS
capital goods (machinery etc.)
1,329
cotton
783
72
97
98
129
135 145 161 170
textiles
cement
edible oil
fertilizers
wheat
yarn
crude petroleum
petroleum products

frozen prawns/frogs'legs
jute goods
leather/leather products
ready-made clothes
272 198 168
raw jute
MAJOR IMPORTS AND EXPORTS, 1994 (US$ million)
1,292
38 57
tea
EXPORTS

▼ This is the largest and most costly fertilizer factory in Bangladesh. It opened in Chittagong in 1995 and cost US$ 510 million.

calculated on a yearly basis. Thus the longer it takes to repay a loan, the higher will be the final amount paid. Inevitably, all the obstacles hindering the country's progress have also delayed the repayment of loans. A point has now been reached where Bangladesh's future is being damaged by debt, and the money that was supposed to help Bangladesh is, in fact, harming it. The best way for this financial burden to be removed is to consider the money as a gift. However, foreign governments and organizations are reluctant to write off these debts.

■ TRANSPORT

The numerous rivers, and the huge seasonal variation in their widths and depths, has prevented the development of roads and railways in Bangladesh. Because building bridges is too costly, ferries have to be used frequently. This means that journeys by road or rail take a long time and monsoon floods can make them impossible.

RIVER TRAVEL

Most people and goods travel by water. Large and small passenger boats shuttle up and down and across the rivers, taking people to work and to visit families and friends. Small cargo ships distribute imported goods from Chittagong to Khulna and Dhaka, returning laden with export cargo to Mongla, where it is loaded on to ocean-going ships. The busy routes get so cluttered with craft of all shapes and sizes that it is easy to see why the rivers are

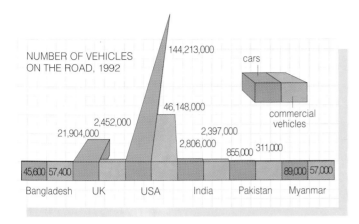

NUMBER OF VEHICLES
ON THE ROAD, 1992

144,213,000

cars

commercial
vehicles

46,148,000

2,452,000

21,904,000

2,397,000
2,806,000

855,000   311,000

45,600 57,400

89,000 57,000

| Bangladesh | UK | USA | India | Pakistan | Myanmar |

◀ *Small ferries
take people
across rivers.*

▶ *Cheap, clean
and colourful,
some of Dhaka's
huge number of
rickshaws.*

◀ *These motorized rickshaws and
buses carry people to the outskirts of
Chittagong.*

referred to as the watery highways of
Bangladesh. During the rainy months,
8,000 kilometres of them can be used by
medium to large-sized boats. A further
18,000 kilometres are open to small boats.
In the dry season, the NAVIGABLE length of
the rivers shrinks by half.

URBAN TRANSPORT

There are many bicycles and motorbikes in
Bangladesh, but only the richest people
own cars. Most people rely on public
transport to get about. Pedal-powered
rickshaws are the most common, and
cheapest, method of transport around
towns and cities. They can carry a family of
four for very little cost. Rickshaws can also
be converted into freight-carriers. They
have become an indispensable part of

Dhaka's transport system, carrying about
5 per cent of the city's freight. They are
also a mini-industry, that provides work for
thousands. In 1997, there were about
200,000 rickshaws in Dhaka, more than in
any other city in the world. One machine
provides a job for two drivers, each one
working a nine-hour shift. In addition, there
are estimated to be 100,000 people
involved in repairing and manufacturing
bits and pieces for rickshaws. As well as
bringing all these advantages, rickshaws
help to reduce Dhaka's vehicle pollution
levels. Although a little more expensive
than rickshaws, buses are usually
crammed, especially during the rush hours.
Taxis are the most expensive form of urban
transport and are only used by the wealthy
or by people in a hurry.

◀ *Few Bangladeshis can afford to travel by their national airline.*

RAIL AND AIR

The railways have been neglected for a long time, so the carriages are old and dilapidated, and the engines often break down. Bangladeshis prefer to travel across country by more reliable buses and

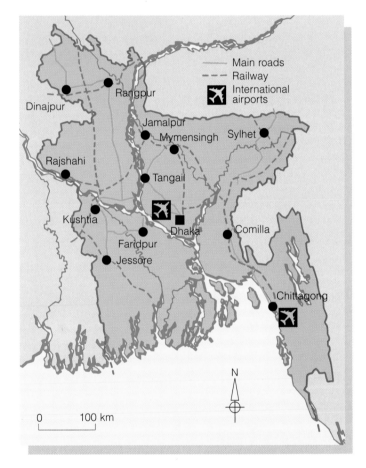

KEY FACTS

● In 1992, there were 13,627 kilometres of roads, 8,546 kilometres of which were paved.
● The most common means of motorized transport in Bangladesh is the motorcycle. In 1995, there were 134,303 of them.
● There are 8,433 kilometres of inland waterways which can be used for transport.
● In 1992, there were 2,892 kilometres of railways and 502 stations.
● 55 million people and 2.5 million tonnes of freight are carried on the railways each year in 20,142 carriages and wagons.
● Biman Bangladesh Airlines carried 667,000 passengers in 1993.
● The first rickshaw arrived in Dhaka in 1938 from Calcutta.
● The first proper bridge across the River Jamuna has just been completed. It cost US$ 700 million.
● The width of the River Jamuna varies from 2.5 kilometres during the dry months to 15 kilometres during the wet ones.

minibuses, even though there are long waits at ferry crossings, and the poor roads make travel uncomfortable.

The quickest, and also the most expensive, way around Bangladesh is on the aircraft of the small national airline, Biman. It connects all the main cities with regular flights. Its planes also fly from Dhaka to many other countries.

THE ENVIRONMENT

THE WESTERN DELTA

In the early 1960s, India constructed the Farakka Dam across the River Ganges near the border with Bangladesh. It was designed to increase the amount of water flowing down the Hooghly river, a tributary of the Ganges, which was silting up. While this helped to lower the amount of water entering Bangladesh during the monsoon, it also meant that the Ganges was emptier during the dry season.

The western half of Bangladesh was the worst affected. As its rivers shrunk, the tide was able to push its way inland, filling the channels and underground reserves with seawater. The salt poisoned crops and drinking water. The west is also the driest part of Bangladesh, so its farmers rely on IRRIGATION. With little freshwater available for their fields, the soil turned to dust which was easily blown away.

In 1985, a water-sharing agreement was made between India and Bangladesh to halt the damage being done by the Farakka Dam. The government of Bangladesh also began building a network of irrigation canals. These will distribute water from the Ganges around the western delta to bring it alive again.

POLLUTED WATER

As raw sewage enters the rivers without being treated, the rivers contain a lot of germs. Industrial waste, often full of harmful chemicals, is also pumped directly

▼ *Potatoes being harvested in the dry soil of the western delta.*

into them. Since the Green Revolution, chemicals have drained off farmland treated with fertilizers and pesticides. Freshwater fish form an important part of Bangladeshis' diet. Not only is the polluted river water killing fish, people are concerned that eating them may be harming their health.

Pollution is at its worst along the coast near Chittagong. Here oil tankers cleaning out their tanks have added to factory waste, creating a lethal combination of chemicals which has nearly 'killed' the sea.

Naturally the government is very concerned, but it does not have the money to build sufficient water-treatment plants to deal with the problem. Also, new anti-pollution laws are having little effect because corrupt officials are turning a blind eye to waste-dumpers.

KEY FACTS

● Bangladesh is home to 250 species of mammals, 200 kinds of fish, 150 varieties of reptiles and amphibians, and 750 types of birds.
● The Asian Development Bank plans to provide US$ 5 million in aid, in order to lower the pollution of the inland and coastal waters.
● Because the land in Bangladesh is so low, global warming would have catastrophic consequences if it were to cause a rise in the level of the world's oceans.

◀ *These plastic bottles will be recycled into new ones.*

▶ *The Royal Bengal tiger was once nearly killed off by hunters. It lives in the Sundarbans, which is now a national park. It is a tidal region with many mudflats and mangrove swamps. Since it is not an easy place for people to travel around in, no one knows how many tigers are now living there, although their numbers are increasing.*

WILDLIFE

Many species of animals and birds can be seen in Bangladesh, especially in the thick forests of the Sundarbans and the Chittagong Hill Tracts. The hills are home to elephants, leopards, deer, monkeys, parakeets and mynah birds. But the animal Bangladesh is most proud of is the Royal Bengal tiger which lives in the Sundarbans. This has been turned into a national park where the Bengal tiger can live without being hunted to extinction.

◉ THE FUTURE

Taking into account all its problems, Bangladesh has done remarkably well for a poor country. A rapidly expanding population used to put an enormous strain on its limited resources. It is now growing at 1.8 per cent a year, down from a figure of 2.6 per cent. This is a significant decrease for which women are largely responsible. Generally better informed and more confident about themselves, they have been instrumental in nearly halving the average size of families: from seven to four children.

With the help of self-help organizations like the Grameen Bank and the Bangladesh Rural Advancement Committee (BRAC), women are spearheading a social revolution in the countryside. The Grameen Bank and BRAC provide low-interest loans to women's groups. The money is channelled through women because past behaviour has shown that they are more reliable at repaying loans than men. The Grameen Bank, for example, has supported the building of 300,000 new homes. BRAC helps to run 28,000 village schools.

Dealing with environmental problems has been more challenging. Cyclones cannot be stopped. However, with the help

▼ *A social worker tells rural women about the benefits of pumped water over dirty river water.*

KEY FACTS

● In 1998, better healthcare and diet mean that people live 16 years longer and 54 fewer babies die out of every 1,000 born, compared to 1960.

● In 1998, the Grameen Bank began to provide every village with a mobile pay-phone.

● Since 1993, with help from abroad, 650 cyclone shelters have been built.

▶ *These women run a savings scheme in their village. Here, they are being advised by a Grameen Bank worker.*

of satellites and radio broadcasts, the coastal inhabitants now receive advance warning of their arrival and they can take shelter. The Himalaya Mountains are outside Bangladesh, but their DEFORESTATION has caused SOIL EROSION. This has blocked up the delta's rivers and made them more prone to flooding. A multi-million dollar flood-control plan, financed from abroad, has been under way since the early 1990s. Hundreds of kilometres of river banks will be strengthened and raised, but there is little agreement on whether this will reduce the flooding or make it worse.

Even if nature can be tamed, future progress depends on governments providing stability. This will attract foreign firms. With foreign investment, Bangladesh can provide more jobs and increase its exports to pay off crippling debts. It is the poorest who suffer the worst and who would benefit the most from a more prosperous Bangladesh. The Bangladeshis have an amazing capacity to bounce back from disaster and rebuild their lives. They are working hard for a higher standard of living in the future.

FURTHER INFORMATION

● LEEDS DEVELOPMENT EDUCATION CENTRE
151–153 Cardigan Road, Leeds LS6 1LJ
Provides a teaching pack, Dhaka to Dundee, contrasting the lives of people in Scotland and Bangladesh.

● ACTION AID
3 Church Street, Frome, Somerset BA11 1PW
Provides a teaching pack, Economic Issues Facing Bangladesh, and a video, People of the Delta.

● OXFAM
274 Banbury Road, Oxford OX2 7DZ
Provides a teaching pack, Creating Art, Creating Income: a women's textile workshop in Bangladesh.

● CAFOD
Romero Close, Stockwell Road
London SW9 9TY
Provides a teaching pack, Working in Partnership in Bangladesh.

BOOKS ABOUT BANGLADESH
Bangladesh: the Strength to Succeed, Jim Moran, Oxfam 1995 (age 11–16)
Bangladesh, Steve Brace, Wayland 1994 (age 9–14)
The Ganges Delta and Its People, David Cumming, Wayland 1994 (age 9–14)
The Ganges, David Cumming, Wayland 1993 (age 9–14)
World in View: Pakistan and Bangladesh, Nicholas Nugent, Heinemann 1992 (age 9–14)

GLOSSARY

COUP
A violent or illegal change in government.

DEFORESTATION
The cutting down of large numbers of trees, leaving the land bare.

EXPORT EARNINGS
Money earned from selling things abroad.

FERTILIZERS
Nutrients added to the soil that help plants to grow. These are usually chemicals, but there are also natural fertilizers, like animal dung.

INTEREST
Money that has to be paid in return for being given a loan. This is in the form of a percentage of the amount originally borrowed.

IRRIGATION
The process of bringing water to farmland by means of pumps, canals, channels or ditches.

NAVIGABLE
A word used to describe a river deep enough to be used by boats or ships.

PESTICIDES
Chemicals for killing insects harmful to crops.

PULSES
Edible seeds of plants like lentils, beans and peas.

RIVER SYSTEM
A large river and all the smaller ones flowing into it.

SOIL EROSION
The process by which top soil is carried away by the action of the wind or rain.

SUBCONTINENT
A large geographically or politically independent part of a continent.

WORKERS' CO-OPERATIVE
A group of people who work together rather than as individuals.

INDEX

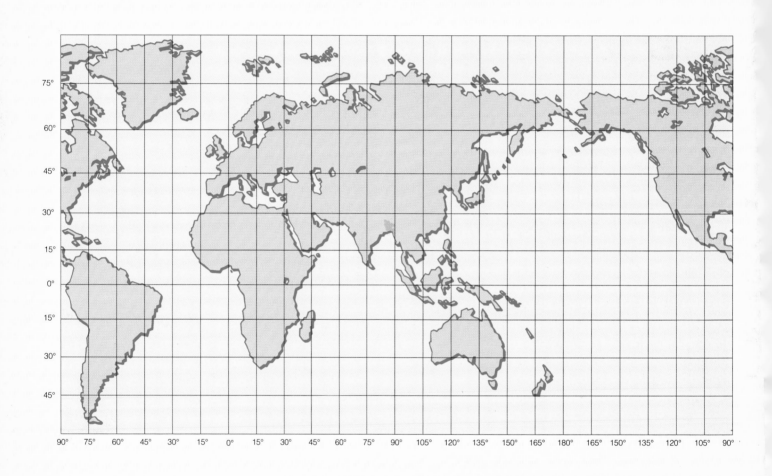